AF263734

Manuel McFeely

BASIC PYTHON COMMANDS

Learn the basic commands of the world's most intuitive and widely used programming language

TABLE OF CONTENTS

INTRODUCTION

Python is a programming language created by Guido Van Rossum in 1991.

Considered a simple language, beautiful to read and see, suitable for beginners, today Python is used in many areas:

- web development with Django and Flask
- data science
- machine learning and computer vision
- scripting
- data manipulation and data mining

According to the latest data, Python is the fastest-growing programming language globally, mainly due to its simplicity and the fact that it is incredibly intuitive.

Python language, in fact, is defined as "interpreted". This means that the Python code you write is read on the fly by a "translator" that turns it into "machine" language, which is a language that only your computer's processor can understand.

The "translator" is a kind of engine inside Python, a tool that reads and interprets our code.

The transition from code to execution is therefore almost immediate.

In addition to interpreted programming languages there are also compiled ones, where the code you write speaks more directly to the machine and must be translated by a tool called a compiler (examples of compiled languages are C, C#, Java).

These languages are much more complicated and laborious than an interpreted language like Python. That's why Python is so successful.

Interpreted languages like Python can be written in a "language" that is very similar to English, which is why Python is said to be high level.

Another example of an interpreted, high-level language is JavaScript.

In addition to being interpreted and high-level, Python is also a dynamic language. This means that when faced with a variable, we can change the variable's contents and the program will accept it without any problems, unlike other languages called static, which do not allow variables to be modified.

Since some years, Python can be transformed into a static language with the so-called type annotations, but this is a more advanced concept that we are not interested in here.

We were talking about the qualities of Python, here is another one: Python is an object-oriented language.

Objects can be anything: a shoe, a dress, a house, a tree... When we take an object from the real world and transport it into Python code, we create an object.

It is said that Python is object-oriented because it is very easy to create new objects and reason about them very conveniently.

One of the most important features of Python, though, is its focus on style.

By style, we mean how information, i.e., commands, are typed. If we type a command correctly, Python will read it and execute it, otherwise, it will give an error signal.

That's why it's essential to know the correct commands to use.

In this manual, you'll find just that: the commands that will let you use your Python at its best.

Chapter 1. PYTHON COMMANDS

THE BASIC PYTHON COMMANDS

The basic commands are as follows.

1. **Comments:** # symbol is used to comments in python. For multiline comments, you'll have to use """ symbols or enclosing the comment in the """ symbol.

Example:
Print "Hello World." # this is the comment section.

Example:
""" This is Hello world project.".

2. **Type function:** These commands are used to determine the type of a variable by utilizing built-in functions.

   Example:

   type (20), its type is int.

   >>> type (20) < type 'int' >

   Example:

   type (-1 +j), its type is complex

   >>> type (-1+j)

   < type 'complex' >

3. **Strings**: It is mainly enclosed in double quotes.

   Example:

   type ("hello World"), type is string

   >>> type ("hello World")

   < type 'str' >

4. **Lists**: Lists are mainly enclosed in square brackets.

    Example:

    type ([1, 2]), type is list

    >>> type ([1, 2, 3])

    < type 'List' >

5. **Tuple**: Tuple is mainly enclosed in parenthesis.

    Example:

    type (1, 2, 3), a type is a tuple.

    >>> type ((1, 2, 3))

    <type 'tuple' >

6. **Range**: This function is used to create the list of integers.

Example:

>>> range (10)

Output: [0, 1, 2, 3, 4, 5, 6, 7, 8, 9]

Example:

>>> range (1,10)

Output: [1, 2, 3, 4, 5, 6, 7, 8, 9]

7. **Boolean values**: This data type helps in retrieving the data in True or false form.

Example:

>>> True

True

>>> type (True)

< type 'bool' >

Example:

>>> False

False

>>> type (False)

< type 'bool' >

8. **Operator**: For different functions such as division, multiplying, adding, and subtracting, different operators are used.

Example:

>>> 16/2

8

Example:

>>> 2 * * ½

1

9. **Variable and assignment**: variable = expression is used in the assignment statement. A single '=' is used for assignment, and for quality testing, a double '= =' is used.

Example:

```
>>> X= 235
>>> print X
235
>>> Z= 2* X
>>> print Z
470
```

10. **Comparison operators**: Used in comparing values, and the result is always a boolean value.

Example:
```
>>> 2 < 3
True
```

Chapter 2. FUNCTIONS IN PYTHON

In programming, functions are used to group a collection of instructions that you want to utilize repeatedly or better self-contained in a sub-program and called as needed due to their complexity. That is, a function is a piece of code that is written to perform a specific task. The function may or may not require several inputs to complete that task. The function may or may not return one or more values when the task is completed.

In Python, there are three categories of functions:

- Built-in functions such as help(), which asks for assistance, min(), which returns the minimum value, print(), which prints an object to the terminal, and so on... An overview containing more of these functions can be found here.
- User-Defined Functions (UDFs), which are functions created by users to assist them;
- Anonymous functions, often known as lambda functions, are not declared using the conventional def keyword.

Techniques vs. Functions

A function that is part of a class is referred to as a technique. A class instance or object accesses it. This restriction does not apply to a function: it just relates to a solo function. This indicates that while all techniques are functions, not all functions are techniques.

Consider this example, where you first define a function plus() and then a Summation class with a sum() technique:

```
script.py                                          IPython Shell
1    # Define a function `plus()`                  In [1]:
2 ▾  def plus(a,b):
3        return a + b
4
5    # Create a `Summation` class
6 ▾  class Summation(object):
7 ▾    def sum(self, a, b):
8          self.contents = a + b
9          return self.contents
```

You must first define an instance or object of the Summation class before calling the sum() function. So, let's make a definition for such an object:

```
script.py                                          IPython Shell
1    # Instantiate `Summation` class to call `sum()`   In [1]:
2    sumInstance = Summation()
3    sumInstance.sum(1,2)
```

Remember that this instantiation isn't required when calling the function plus()! You should be able to execute plus(1,2) without any issues in the DataCamp Light code block!

Arguments vs. Parameters

Parameters are the names given to functions and techniques when they are defined and where arguments are mapped. In other words, arguments are the things that are passed into a function or technique call, whereas the function or technique code refers to the arguments as parameter names.

Consider the following scenario, then return to the DataCamp Light chunk: Even though you created three parameters, self, a, and b, you pass two arguments to the Summation class's sum() technique.

So, what happened to you?

Every class technique's first argument references the class's current instance, which is Summation. This argument is commonly referred to as "self."

Because the self is the parameter name for an implicitly given argument that refers to the instance via which a technique is invoked, you don't pass the reference to self in this situation. It is implicitly placed into the argument list.

User-Defined Functions: How To Define A Function (UDFs)

The following are the four steps to defining a function in Python:

1. Declare the function with the term def, followed by the function name.
2. Add parameters to the function, which should be placed within the function's parentheses. Put a colon at the end of your line.
3. Include statements that the functions should execute.
4. If your function should output something, end it with a return statement. Your function will return None if it doesn't have a return statement.

Of course, as you progress, your functions will become more complex: you can add for loops, flow control, and more to make it more fine-grained:

```python
def hello():
    name = str(input("Enter your name: "))
    if name:
        print ("Hello " + str(name))
    else:
```

```
    print("Hello World")

    return
```

```
hello()
```

You ask the user for a name in the function mentioned above. The function will print "Hello World" if no name is specified. Otherwise, the user will be greeted with a personalized "Hello."

Also, keep in mind that your UDF can have one or more function parameters. When you get to the section on Function Arguments, you'll learn more about this. Furthermore, as a consequence of your function, you can return one or several values.

The statement of return

You don't need to return anything in your UDF hello() because you're printing something. There will be no difference between this function and the one listed above:

```
script.py                                              IPython Shell
1 ▾ def hello_noreturn():                              In [1]: |
2     print("Hello World")
```

If you want to keep working with the result of your function and test out some operations on it, you'll need to use the return statement to return a value, such as a String, an integer, or... Consider the following scenario, in which hello() returns "hello" as a String and hello no return() returns None:

```
script.py                                              IPython Shell
 1 ▾ def hello():                                      In [1]: |
 2      print("Hello World")
 3      return("hello")
 4
 5 ▾ def hello_noreturn():
 6      print("Hello World")
 7
 8    # Multiply the output of `hello()` with 2
 9    hello() * 2
10
11    # (Try to) multiply the output of `hello_noreturn()` with
      2
12    hello_noreturn() * 2
```

Because you can't do anything with a None, the second technique returns an error. You'll get a TypeError saying that the multiplication operation for NoneType (the None returned by hello no return()) and int isn't possible (2).

When a function encounters a return statement, it exits immediately, even if that implies it won't return any value:

```
script.py                                      IPython Shell
1 ▾ def run():                                 In [1]:
2 ▾     for x in range(10):
3 ▾         if x == 2:
4               return
5       print("Run!")
6
7   run()
```

When working with the return statement, it's also worth noting that you can utilize it to return multiple values. Tuples are used to do this.

Keep in mind that this data structure is similar to a list in that it can have many values. On the other hand, Tuples are immutable, which means you can't change the amounts contained in them! You put it together using double parentheses (). The comma and the assignment operator can be used to unpack tuples into numerous variables.

To see how your function can return several values, consider the following example:

```
script.py                                                IPython Shell
1    # Define `plus()`                                    In [1]:
2    def plus(a,b):
3        sum = a + b
4        return (sum, a)
5
6    # Call `plus()` and unpack variables
7    sum, a = plus(3,4)
8
9    # Print `sum()`
10   print(sum)
```

Return sum, a would have the same outcome as return (sum, a), because of the former pack's sum and an into a tuple behind the hood!

What Should A Function Be Called?

You've already seen a lot of examples of how to call a function in the previous sections. When you call a function, you're telling Python to run the function you've specified, either directly through another function or from the Python prompt (as explained in the section "Nested Functions").

Simply execute hello() to invoke your newly defined function, as shown in the DataCamp Light chunk below:

```
script.py                                                IPython Shell
1    hello()                                              In [1]:
```

How Do I Include Docstrings In A Python Function?

Another important part of writing Python functions is the use of docstrings. Docstrings define your function's behavior, such as the computations it conducts and the results it returns. These descriptions act as documentation for your function, allowing anyone who reads the docstring of your function to understand what it does without having to read the entire function definition.

Function docstrings are inserted in the line immediately following the function header, between triple quotation marks. 'Prints "Hello World"' is an adequate Docstring for your hello() technique.

```python
def hello():
"Prints "Hello World."

Returns:
    None
"""

    print("Hello World")
    return
```

It's worth noting that docstrings can be much longer than the one shown here. If you want to learn more about docstrings, go to the Github repositories of Python libraries like sci-kit-learn or pandas, where you'll find many examples!

Python Function Arguments

You studied the distinction between parameters and arguments earlier. In a nutshell, arguments are the items passed to any function or technique call, whereas the technique or function code refers to the arguments as parameter names. Python UDFs can take four different types of arguments:

- Keyword arguments
- Variable number of arguments
- Default arguments
- Required arguments

Default Arguments

If no value is specified as an argument during the function call, the default parameter is used. To assign this default value, use the assignment operator =, as illustrated in the following example:

```
script.py                                    IPython Shell
1    # Define `plus()` function              In [1]:
2 ▾  def plus(a,b = 2):
3        return a + b
4
5    # Call `plus()` with only `a` parameter
6    plus(a=1)
7
8    # Call `plus()` with `a` and `b` parameters
9    plus(a=1, b=3)
```

Required Arguments

The required arguments of a UDF, as the name implies, are those that must be present. These arguments must be given during the function call and in the correct order, as seen in the example below:

```python
# script.py                                    IPython Shell
1  # Define 'plus()' with required arguments    In [1]:
2  def plus(a,b):
3      return a + b
```

To call the function without encountering any problems, you'll need arguments that map to the a and b parameters. The outcome won't change if you swap a and b around, but it might if you modify plus() to the following:

```python
# script.py                                    IPython Shell
1  # Define 'plus()' with required arguments    In [1]:
2  def plus(a,b):
3      return a/b
```

Keyword Arguments

You can utilize keyword arguments in your function call to ensure that you call all of the parameters in the correct order. These are used to identify arguments based on their parameter names. To make this more evident, consider the following example:

It's worth noting that you may use the keyword arguments to change the order of the parameters and still obtain the same result when you run your function:

```
script.py                                             IPython Shell
1   # Define `plus()` function                        In [1]:
2 ▾ def plus(a,b):
3      return a + b
4
5   # Call `plus()` function with keyword arguments
6   plus(b=2, a=1)
```

Variable Number of Arguments

You can make use of the following syntax with *args if you don't know the precise amount of arguments you want to provide to a function:

```
script.py                                                          IPython Shell
1   # Define `plus()` function to accept a variable number of      In [1]:
    arguments
2 ▾ def plus(*args):
3       return sum(args)
4
5   # Calculate the sum
6   plus(1,4,5)
```

An asterisk (*) is put before the variable name that carries the values of all non keyword variable parameters, an asterisk (*) is put. Note that you might have called the addition() function *variant, *var int args, or any other name.

Replace *args with a different name that includes an asterisk. You'll notice that the code above continues to work!

You can see how the above program uses the built-in Python sum() function to add up all of the arguments supplied to plus (). If you want to avoid this and create the function totally from scratch, you can use this technique:

```
script.py                                                    IPython Shell
1    # Define 'plus()' function to accept a variable number of   In [1]:
     arguments
2 ▾  def plus(*args):
3        total = 0
4 ▾      for i in args:
5            total += i
6        return total
7
8    # Calculate the sum
9    plus(20,30,40,50)
```

Global vs. Local Variables

Variables specified inside a function body have a local scope, while variables defined outside the function body have a global scope. Local variables are defined within a function block and can only be retrieved within that function, but global variables are accessible by all functions in your script:

```
script.py                                                          IPython Shell
1    # Global variable `init`                                       In [1]:
2    init = 1
3
4    # Define `plus()` function to accept a variable number of
     arguments
5 ▾  def plus(*args):
6      # Local variable `sum()`
7      total = 0
8 ▾    for i in args:
9          total += i
10     return total
11
12   # Access the global variable
13   print("this is the initialized value " + str(init))
14
15   # (Try to) access the local variable
16   print("this is the sum " + str(total))
```

When you try to print out all the local variable total defined inside the function body, you'll get a NameError that indicates the name 'total' is not defined. On the other hand, the init variable can be printed without difficulty.

Python Anonymous Functions

In Python, anonymous functions are sometimes known as lambda functions since they are declared with the lambda keyword rather than the conventional def keyword.

```
script.py                                          IPython Shell
  1   double = lambda x: x*2                        In [1]:
  2
  3   double(5)
```

The unnamed or lambda method in the DataCamp Light chunk is lambda x: x*2. The parameter is x, and then evaluated, and returned expression or instruction is x*2. In contrast to the samples, you saw in the first part of this functions tutorial, this function does not have a name. If the above code had to be written as a UDF, it would look like this:

```
def double(x):
    return x*2
```

Consider the following example of a lambda function that takes two arguments:

```
script.py                                          IPython Shell
1   # `sum()` lambda function                      In [1]:
2   sum = lambda x, y: x + y;
3
4   # Call the `sum()` anonymous function
5   sum(4,5)
6
7   # "Translate" to a UDF
8 ▪ def sum(x, y):
9       return x+y
```

When you need a nameless function for a brief length of time that is produced at runtime, you use anonymous functions. When working with filter(), map(), and reduce(), this is especially important:

```
script.py                                                    IPython Shell
1    from functools import reduce                             In [1]:
2
3    my_list = [1,2,3,4,5,6,7,8,9,10]
4
5    # Use lambda function with `filter()`
6    filtered_list = list(filter(lambda x: (x*2 > 10), my_list
     ))
7
8    # Use lambda function with `map()`
9    mapped_list = list(map(lambda x: x*2, my_list))
10
11   # Use lambda function with `reduce()`
12   reduced_list = reduce(lambda x, y: x+y, my_list)
13
14   print(filtered_list)
15   print(mapped_list)
16   print(reduced_list)
```

The filter() function, as the name implies, filters the original input list my list using a criterion of >10. Using map(), you can apply a function to all entries in the list my list. All elements are multiplied by 2 in this scenario.

The reduce() technique is included in the functools library. This function is applied cumulatively to the entries in my list from left to right, reducing the sequence to a single value, in this case, 55.

Main () is used as a function.

If you've worked with other programming languages, such as Java, you'll know that the main function is essential for functions to be executed. This isn't required for Python, as you can see from the examples above. However, incorporating a main() function in your Python program might help you organize your code logically because it contains the most critical components.

You can easily create a main() function and call it the same way you did with the other functions:

```
script.py                                    IPython Shell
1   # Define `main()` function              In [1]:
2 ▾ def main():
3     hello()
4     print("This is a main function")
5
6   main()
```

However, when you import your main() function as a module, the code of your main() technique will be called. When __name__ == '__main__', you call the main() technique to ensure that this does not happen.

As a result, the above code chunk's code becomes:

```
script.py                                              IPython Shell
1   # Define `main()` function                         In [1]:
2 ▾ def main():
3       hello()
4       print("This is a main function")
5
6   # Execute `main()` function
7 ▾ if __name__ == '__main__':
8       main()
```

Aside from the __main__ technique, you also have a __init__ function that initializes a class or object instance. Simply said, it functions as a constructor or initializer and is called automatically whenever a new instance of a class is created. The newly generated object is allocated to the self parameter in that function, which you saw earlier in this course.

Consider the following scenario:

```python
class Dog:
    """

    Requires:
    legs - Legs so that the dog can walk.
    color - A color of the fur.
    """


    def __init__(self, legs, color):
        self.legs = legs
        self.color = color


    def bark(self):
        bark = "bark" * 2
        return bark


if __name__ == "__main__":
    dog = Dog(4, "brown")
    bark = dog.bark()
    print(bark)
```

Chapter 3. DATA TYPES

This tutorial will teach you about the various data types available in Python.

Python has several data types.

In Python, each value has a datatype. Data types are essentially classes, and variables are instances (objects) of these classes because everything in Python programming is an object.

Python has several different data types. The following are some of the more important types.

Numbers in Python

Python numbers include integers, floating-point numbers, and complex numbers. In Python, they are known as int, float, and complex classes.

The type() technique can be used to determine which class a variable or value belongs to. The instance() function is used to determine if an object belongs to a specific class.

```
a = 5
print(a, "is of type", type(a))

a = 2.0
print(a, "is of type", type(a))

a = 1+2j
print(a, "is complex number?", isinstance(1+2j,complex))
```

Output

```
5 is of type <class 'int'>
2.0 is of type <class 'float'>
(1+2j) is complex number? True
```

Integers can have any length; the only limitation is the amount of memory available.

Up to 15 decimal digits, a floating-point number is accurate. Decimal points separate integers and floating points. 1.0 is a floating-point number, while 1 is an integer.

The formula for complex numbers is x + yj, where x is the real and y is the imaginary parts. Here are a few illustrations.

```
>>> a = 12345678901234567891
>>> a
12345678901234567891
>>> b = 0.1234567890123456789
>>> b
0.12345678901234568
>>> c = 1+2j
>>> c
(1+2j)
```

The float variable b has been shortened.

A Python list is a collection of items in a specific order. It is an extremely flexible datatype that is one of the most commonly used in Python. It is not necessary for all items in a list to be of the same type.

Declaring a list is rather simple—commas separate items, which are enclosed in brackets [ ].

```
a = [1, 2.2, 'python']
```

To extract a range of items from a list, we can use the slicing operator [ ]. In Python, the index starts at 0.

```python
a = [5,10,15,20,25,30,35,40]

# a[2] = 15
print("a[2] = ", a[2])

# a[0:3] = [5, 10, 15]
print("a[0:3] = ", a[0:3])

# a[5:] = [30, 35, 40]
print("a[5:] = ", a[5:])
```

Output

```
a[2] =   15
a[0:3] =   [5, 10, 15]
a[5:] =   [30, 35, 40]
```

Lists are changeable, which means that the value of a list's elements can be changed.

```python
a = [1, 2, 3]
a[2] = 4
print(a)
```

Output

```
[1, 2, 4]
```

Tuple in Python

A tuple, like a list, is an ordered series of elements. Tuples vary solely in that they are immutable. Tuples can't be changed once they've been generated.

Tuples are used to write-protect data and because they do not alter dynamically.

It is defined within parenthesis (), with commas between the pieces.

```
t = (5,'program', 1+3j)
```

We can extract things with the slicing operator [], but we can't change its value.

```
t = (5,'program', 1+3j)

# t[1] = 'program'
print("t[1] = ", t[1])

# t[0:3] = (5, 'program', (1+3j))
print("t[0:3] = ", t[0:3])

# Generates error
# Tuples are immutable
t[0] = 10
```

```
t[1] =  program
t[0:3] =  (5, 'program', (1+3j))
Traceback (most recent call last):
  File "test.py", line 11, in <module>
    t[0] = 10
TypeError: 'tuple' object does not support item assignment
```

Strings in Python are a collection of Unicode characters. To represent strings, we can use single or double quotations. Triple quotes, ''' or, "can be used to signify multi-line strings.

```
s = "This is a string"
print(s)
s = '''A multiline
string'''
print(s)
```



```
This is a string
A multiline
string
```

The slicing operator [ ] can be used with strings just like it can with lists and tuples. Strings, on the other hand, are unchangeable.

```python
s = 'Hello world!'

# s[4] = 'o'
print("s[4] = ", s[4])

# s[6:11] = 'world'
print("s[6:11] = ", s[6:11])

# Generates error
# Strings are immutable in Python
s[5] ='d'
```

OUTPUT

```
s[4] =  o
s[6:11] =  world
Traceback (most recent call last):
  File "<string>", line 11, in <module>
TypeError: 'str' object does not support item assignment
```

A Python Set is an unsorted collection of one-of-a-kind things. Values separated by commas inside braces define a set. The items in a set aren't ordered in any particular sequence.

```python
The # data type of variable a
print(type(a))
```

Output

```
a =  {1, 2, 3, 4, 5}
<class 'set'>
```

On two sets, we can perform set operations such as union and intersection. Sets have their own set of values. They get rid of the duplicates.

```
a = {1,2,2,3,3,3}
print(a)
```

Output

```
{1, 2, 3}
```

Indexing has no value for sets because they are an unordered collection. As a result, the slicing operator [] is useless.

```
>>> a = {1,2,3}
>>> a[1]
Traceback (most recent call last):
  File "<string>", line 301, in runcode
  File "<interactive input>", line 1, in <module>
TypeError: 'set' object does not support indexing
```

Chapter 4. PYTHON SET AND BOOLEANS WITH SYNTAX

We've covered a variety of Python data types so far. Strings, numbers, lists, tuples, and dictionaries were among the objects we worked with.

We've also discovered that declaring the type of data while defining it isn't necessary. Python set examples, and Python Booleans will be discussed today.

Then, in subsequent lectures, we'll look at python functions.

What are Python Sets?

We'll start using Python sets. In Python, a set is a collection of values. It is sequenced, but indexing is not possible.

As we progress through the book with the Python set, we will better understand this. Examples.

1. Creating a Python Set

You must type a sequence of elements separated by commas inside curly brackets to declare a set. Assign it to a Python variable after that.

```
>>> a={1,3,2}
```

We wrote it in the order 1, 3, 2, as you can see. We'll access this set in point b and see what we receive.

Values of many types can be found in a set.

```
>>> c={1,2.0,'three'}
```

a. Elements that are duplicates

There can't be any duplicate elements in a set. Let's try duplicating elements in another set and then accessing it from point b.

```
>>> b={3,2,1,2}
```

b. Flexibility

A set can contain mutable things like a list, set, or even

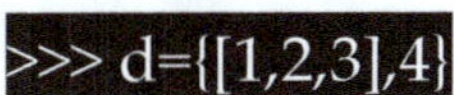

a dictionary, but it cannot contain mutable elements.

```
>>> d={[1,2,3],4}
```

Output

There isn't such thing as a nested Python set, as we explained earlier.

```
>>> d={{1,3,2},4}
```

Output

```
Traceback (most recent call last):File "<pyshell#10>", line 1, in <module>
d={{1,3,2},4}
TypeError: unhashable type: 'set'
```

c. The Python set() function

You can create a set with the set() function.

```
>>> d=set()
```

```
>>> type(d)
```

Output

```
<class 'set'>
```

This produces a set object that is empty. It's important to remember that if you define an empty set like this, you're declaring an empty dictionary, not an empty set. Using the type() technique, we can verify this.

```
>>> d={}
```

```
>>> type(d)
```

Output

```
<class 'set'>
```

However, the set() function can also take a single argument. It should be a list-like iterable.

```
>>> d=set([1,3,2])
```

2. Using Python to Access a Set

Because Python sets do not support indexing, you can only access the complete set at once. Let's see if we can go to the sets from point a.

```
>>> a
```

Output

```
{1, 2, 3}
```

Did you see how the elements were rearranged in ascending order? Now let's see if we can get into set c.

```
>>> c
```

Output

```
{1, 2.0, 'three'}
```

Finally, let's access set b.

```
>>> b
```

Output

```
{1, 2, 3}
```

As you see, we had two 2s when we declared the set, but now we only have one; therefore, it reordered the set automatically.

Sets can't be sliced because they don't support indexing. Let's see if we can slice one.

```
>>> b[1:]
```

Output

```
Traceback (most recent call last):File "<pyshell#26>", line 1, in <module>

b[1:]

TypeError: 'set' object is not subscriptable
```

A set object is not subscribable, as seen in the error.

3. Deleting a Set in Python

You can't delete an element using its index because a set isn't indexed. As a result, one of the approaches listed below must be used.

A technique must be invoked on a set, and it can change the set. Let's start with a collection of numbers for the following cases.

```
>>> numbers={3,2,1,4,6,5}
```

```
>>> numbers
```

Output

```
{1, 2, 3, 4, 5, 6}
```

a. discard()

This technique takes the item to delete as an argument.

```
>>> numbers.discard(3)
```

```
>>> numbers
```

Output

```
{1, 2, 4, 5, 6}
```

Item 3 has been eliminated, as you see in the resulting set.

b. remove()

Like the discard() technique, remove() deletes an item
from the set.

```
>>> numbers.remove(5)
```

```
>>> numbers
```

Output

```
{1, 2, 4, 6}
```

- **discard() vs remove()-**

These two procedures may appear to be identical, yet
there is a distinction.

Discard() ignores an item that doesn't exist in the set,
yet remove() throws a KeyError.

```
>>> numbers.discard(7)
```

```
>>> numbers
```

Output

```
{1, 2, 4, 6}
```

```
>>> numbers.remove(7)
```

Output

```
Traceback (most recent call last):File "<pyshell#37>", line 1, in <module>
numbers.remove(7)
KeyError: 7
```

c. pop ()

On a set, you can use the pop() technique in the same way that you can on a dictionary. It does not, however, take a counter-argument in this case.

There is no way to supply an index to the pop technique because a set does not permit indexing. As a result, it produces a random item.

Furthermore, the item that was popped is printed.

>>> numbers.pop()

Output
1

Let's try popping not/her element.

```
    1.    >>> numbers.pop ()
```

Output

2

Let's give it a shot on another set.

>>> {2,1,3}.pop()

Output
1

d. clear()

Like the pop technique(), the clear() technique for a dictionary can also be applied to a Python set. It empties the set in Python.

```
>>> numbers.clear()
```

```
>>> numbers
```

Output

```
set()
```

As you can see, set() was used to represent an empty set rather than.

4. Using Python to Update a Set

A Python set is mutable, as we've seen. However, as we've shown, we can't utilize indices to reassign it.

```
>>> numbers={3,1,2,4,6,5}
```

```
>>> numbers[3]
```

Output

```
Traceback (most recent call last):File "<pyshell#56>", line 1, in <module>
numbers[3]
TypeError: 'set' object does not support indexing
```

As a result, we employ two techniques for this: add() and update() (). The update() technique has been used on tuples, lists, and strings.

a. include ()

It takes the item to be added to the set as an argument.

```
1.    >>> numbers.add(3.5)
2.    >>> numbers
```

Output

```
{1, 2, 3, 4, 5, 6, 3.5}
```

When you add an existing item to a set, it has no effect on the rest of the set.

```
1.      >>> numbers.add(4)
2.      >>> numbers
```

Output

```
{1, 2, 3, 4, 5, 6, 3.5}
```

b. update()

This technique accepts several inputs and can add numerous items to the set at once.

```
1.      >>> numbers.update([7,8],{1,2,9})
2.      >>> numbers
```

Output

```
{1, 2, 3, 4, 5, 6, 3.5, 7, 8, 9}
```

As can be seen, we might pass a list and a set as parameters. This is because this is not the same as making a set.

5. Python Set Functions

A function is a code that can be applied to a Python set and execute operations on it before returning a value. Let us go over several of the functions that a set can perform.

For demonstration reasons, we'll take a new set.

```
1.   >>> days={'Monday','Tuesday','Wednesday','Thursday','Friday','Saturday','Sunday'}
```

a. len()

The length of a set is returned by the len() method. This is the total number of elements.

```
1.    >>> len(days)
```

Output

```
7
```

b. max()

This function returns the highest-valued item from the set.

```
1.    >>> max({3,1,2})
```

A similar analogy may be made with strings.

```
1.    >>> max(days)
```

Output

```
'Wednesday'
```

Because W has the greatest ASCII value among M, T, W, F, and S, the Python technique returned 'Wednesday.'

However, we are unable to compare values of different types.

```
>>> max({1,2,'three','Three'})
```

Output

```
Traceback (most recent call last):File "<pyshell#69>", line 1, in <module>
max({1,2,'three','Three'})
TypeError: '>' not supported between instances of 'str' and 'int'
```

c. min()

The min() function, like the max() function, returns the lowest-valued item in the Python set.

>>> min(days)'

Output

'Friday'

F has the lowest ASCII value among M, T, W, F, and S.

d. sum()

The sum() function in Python set returns the arithmetic sum of all the items in a set.

```
>>> sum({1,2,3})
```

Output

6

However, you can not apply it to a set that contains strings.

```
>>> sum(days)
```

Output

```
Traceback (most recent call last):File "<pyshell#72>", line 1, in <module>
sum(days)
TypeError: unsupported operand type(s) for +: 'int' and 'str'
```

e. any()

Even if a single item in the set does have a Boolean value of True, this function returns True.

```
False
```

```
1.    >>> any({0,'0'})
```

Output

```
True
```

f. all()

Unlike the any() function, all() evaluates To true only if the Boolean value of all items in the Python set is True. Otherwise, False is returned.

```
>>> all({0,'0'})
```

Output

```
False
```

```
>>> all(days)
```

Output

```
True
```

g. sorted()

The sorted() function will return a Python set to the list that is sorted. It is recomputed, but the original set is unaffected.

```
1.    >>> numbers={1, 2, 3, 4, 5, 6, 3.5}
2.    >>> sorted(numbers)
```

Output

```
[1, 2, 3, 3.5, 4, 5, 6]
```

6. Python Sets Techniques

A technique, unlike a function in a Python set, can change the state of a set. It must be called on a set to conduct a sequence of operations on it.

We've covered the techniques add(), clear(), discard(), pop(), remove(), and update thus far (). More techniques will now be presented from a mathematical standpoint.

a. union()

The union operation is performed on two or more Python sets with this technique. It returns all of the objects that are part of any of those sets.

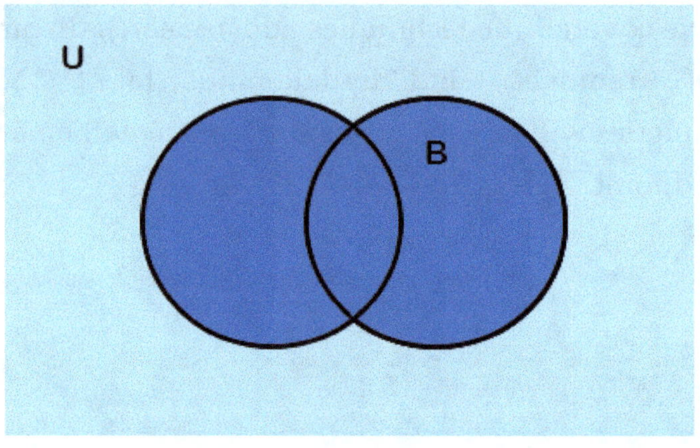

Union in Python Set

```
>>> set1,set2,set3={1,2,3},{3,4,5},{5,6,7}
>>> set1.union(set2,set3)
Output
{1, 2, 3, 4, 5, 6, 7}
>>> set1
Output
{1, 2, 3}
```

Set1 was not changed, as you can see. In Python, a technique does not always change a set.

b. intersection()

This technique accepts sets as an argument and returns the things that are common to all of them.

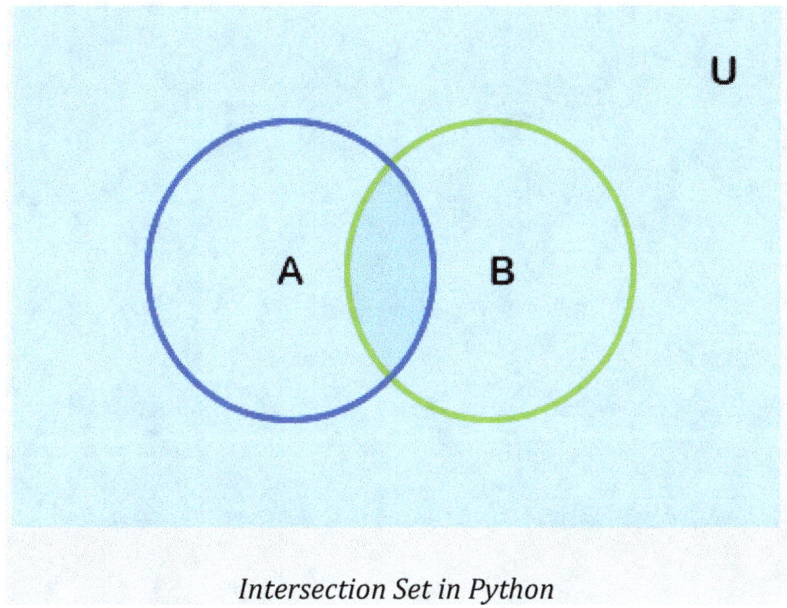

Intersection Set in Python

```
>>> set2.intersection(set1)
```

Output

```
{3}
```

Let's intersect all three sets.

```
>>> set2.intersection(set1,set3)
```

Output

```
set()
```

Because these three sets had nothing in common, it returned an empty set.

c. difference()

The difference() technique compares two or more sets and returns the difference. It gives you a set of results.

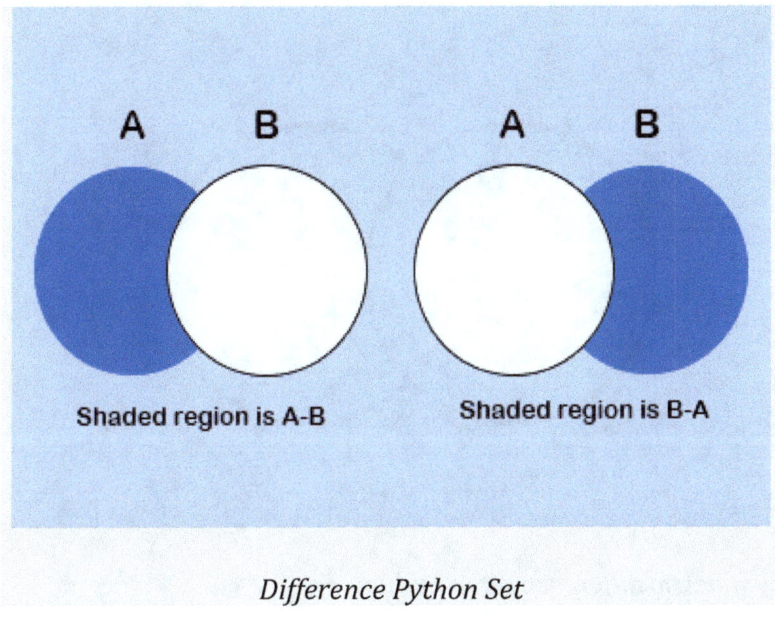

Difference Python Set

```
>>> set1.difference(set2)
```

Output

{1, 2}

This returns the items that are in set1, but not in set2.

```
>>> set1.difference(set2,set3)
```

Output

{1, 2}

d. symmetric_difference()

This technique returns all the items that are unique to each set.

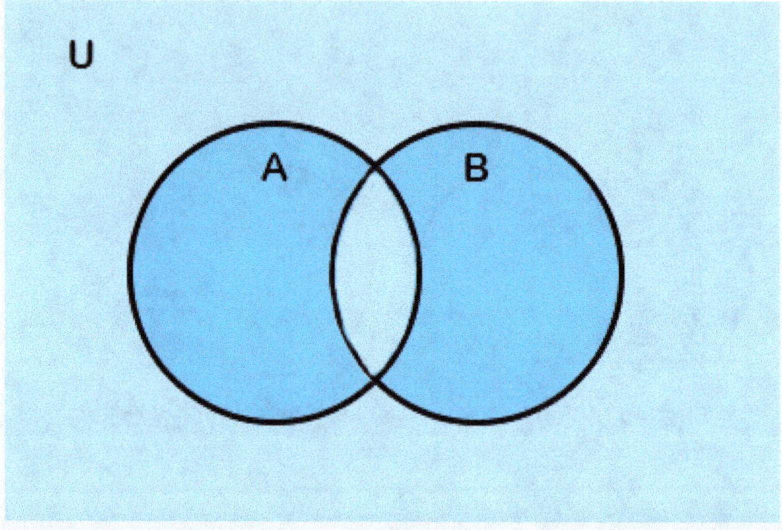

Symmetric difference set in Python

```
>>> set1.symmetric_difference(set2)
```

Output

```
{1, 2, 4, 5}
```

And they're in set1, but not set2; it returned 1 and 2. It also returned 4 and 5, which are in set2 but not in set1. Because it exists in both sets, it did not return 3.

e. intersection update()

It doesn't update the set on which it is called, as we saw with intersection(). The intersection update() technique is used for this.

>>> set1.intersection_update(set2)

>>> set1

Output
```
{3}
```

It only stored 3 in set1 because that was the only thing set1 and set2 had in common.

f. difference update ()

This technique, like intersection-update(), adds the difference to the Python set.

>>> set1={1,2,3}

>>> set2={3,4,5}

>>> set1.difference_update(set2)

>>> set1

Output
```
{1, 2}
```

g. symmetric_difference_update()

It, like the two procedures before it, updates the set with which it is called with symmetric difference.

>>> set1={1,2,3}

>>> set2={3,4,5}

>>> set1.symmetric_difference_update(set2)

>>> set1

Output

```
{1, 2, 4, 5}
```

h. copy()

The copy() technique creates a shallow copy of the Python set.

```
1.    >>> set4=set1.copy()
2.    >>> set1,set4
```

Output

```
({1, 2, 4, 5}, {1, 2, 4, 5})
```

i. is disjoint()

This technique returns True if 2 sets have a null intersection.

```
>>> {1,3,2}.isdisjoint({4,5,6})
```

Output

```
True
```

However, it can take only one argument.

```
1.    >>> {1,3,2}.isdisjoint({3,4,5},{6,7,8})
```

Output

```
Traceback (most recent call last):File "<pyshell#111>", line 1, in <module>
{1,3,2}.isdisjoint({3,4,5},{6,7,8})
TypeError: isdisjoint() takes exactly one argument (2 given)
```

j. issubset()

This technique returns true if the set in the argument contains this set.

```
1.    >>> {1,2}.issubset({1,2,3})
```

Output

```
True
```

```
1.    >>> {1,2}.issubset({1,2})
```

Output

```
True
```

k. issuperset()

Like the issubset() technique, this one returns True if the set contains the set in the argument.

```
>>> {1,3,4}.issuperset({1,2})
```

Output

```
False
```

```
>>> {1,3,4}.issuperset({1})
```

Output

```
True
```

7. Python Set Operations

We'll now look at the operations that can be applied to sets.

a. Membership

The python operators 'in' and 'not in' can be used on elements in a set. This tells us if they're part of the set.

```
>>> 'p' in {'a','p','p','l','e'}
```

Output

```
True
```

```
>>> 0 not in {'0','1'}
```

Output

```
True
```

8. Iterating on a Set in Python

We can iterate on a set in a for-loop just like we can with lists and tuples.

>>> **for** i **in** {1,3,2}:

print(i)

Output

```
12

3
```

Even though the order was 1,3,2, it was printed in ascending order, as you can see.

9. The frozenset

In effect, a frozen set is an immutable set. Its values can't be changed. A set, on the other hand, cannot be used as a dictionary key, although a frozenset may.

>>> {{1,2}:3}

Output

```
Traceback (most recent call last):File "<pyshell#123>", line 1, in <module>
{{1,2}:3}
TypeError: unhashable type: 'set'
```

Now let us try to do this with a frozenset.

```
1.    >>> {frozenset(1,2):3}
```

Output

```
Traceback (most recent call last):File "<pyshell#124>", line 1, in <module>
{frozenset(1,2):3}
TypeError: frozenset expected at most 1 arguments, got 2
```

As you'll see, only one argument is required. Let's look at the proper syntax now.

```
>>> {frozenset([1,2]):3}
```

Output

```
{frozenset({1
```

Booleans in Python?

Booleans

Finally, let's talk about Booleans. A Boolean data type is another Python data type.

1. The value of a Boolean expression

A Boolean value can be either True or False, as we saw earlier. Isalpha() and issubset(), for example, yield a Bo, 2}): 3}

2. Declaring a Boolean expression

You can declare a Boolean in the same way as you would an integer.

d>>> days=True

We didn't need to use quotations to delimit the True value, as you can see. If you do that, you'll get a string instead of a Boolean.

Also, we have reallocated a Boolean to what was previously a set.

>>> type('True')

Output

```
<class 'str'>
```

3. The bool() function

The bool() function, as we've seen before, turns another value into a Boolean type.

>>> bool('Wisdom')

Output

```
True
```

>>> bool([])

Output

```
False
```

4. Different Constructs' Boolean Values

Distinct values have different Boolean equivalents. To find the values in this example, we use the bool() Python set technique.

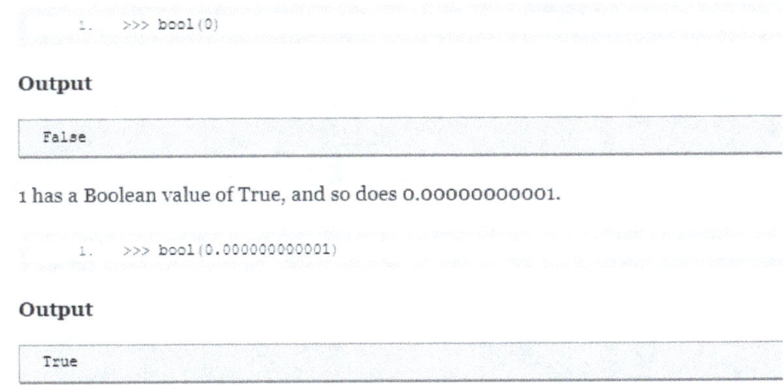

```
1.    >>> bool(0)
```

Output

```
False
```

1 has a Boolean value of True, and so does 0.00000000001.

```
1.    >>> bool(0.000000000001)
```

Output

```
True
```

The Boolean value of 0 is False, for example.

A string has a Boolean value of True, but an empty string has False.

```
>>> bool(' ')
```

Output

True

```
>>> bool('')
```

Output

False

Any empty construct has a Boolean value of False, and a non-empty one has

Output

True.

```
>>> bool(())
Output
False
>>> bool((1,3,2))
Output
True
```

5. Boolean operations

a. Arithmetic algorithm

A set can be subjected to some mathematical operations. It takes a value of 0 for False and 1 for True and then applies the operator to both.

- **Addition**

Two or more Booleans can be added. Let's have a look at how that goes.

>>> **True+False** #1+0

Output
1

>>> **True+True** #1+1

Output
2

>>> **False+True** #0+1

Output
1

>>> **False+False** #0+0

- **Multiplication and Subtraction**

The same method is adopted for multiplication and subtraction.

>>> **False**-True

Output

-1

- **Division**

Let's try dividing Booleans.

>>> **False**/True

Output

0.0

Remember that division results in afloat.

>>> **True**/False

Output

```
Traceback (most recent call last):File "<pyshell#148>", line 1, in <module>
True/False
ZeroDivisionError: division by zero
```

This was a one-time occurrence. In a subsequent session, we'll learn more about exceptions.

- **Exponentiation, Modulus, and Floor Division**

Modulus, exponentiation, and floor division all follow the same laws.

>>> **False%True**

>>> **True****False

Output

```
1
```

>>> **False****False

Output

```
1
```

>>> 0//1

Try your combinations like the one below.

>>> **(True+True)*False**+True

Output

```
1
```

b. Relational

So far, we've learned the relational operators >, <, >=, <=, !=, and ==. All of these things are true for Boolean values.

We will give you a few instances, but you should try them all.

Output

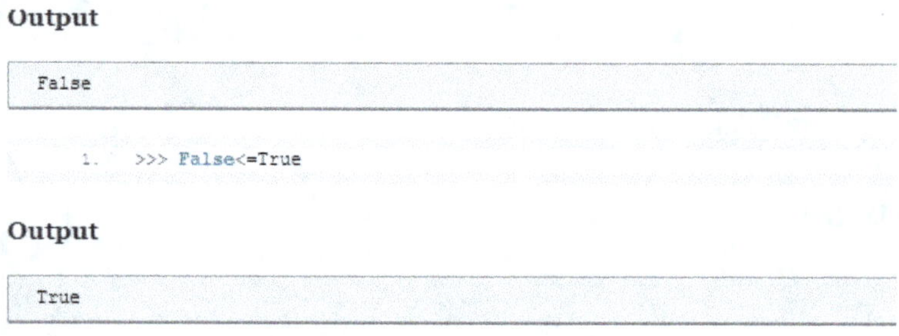

```
False
```

```
1.    >>> False<=True
```

Output

```
True
```

This assumes False has a value of 0 and True has a value of 1.

c. Bitwise

Bitwise operators normally operate bit by bit. The following code, for example, ORs the bits 2(010) and 5(101), yielding 7 as a result (111).

```
>>> 2|5
```

Output

```
7
```

The bitwise operators, on the other hand, also apply to Booleans. Let's have a look at how.

It returns True only if values are True.

Output

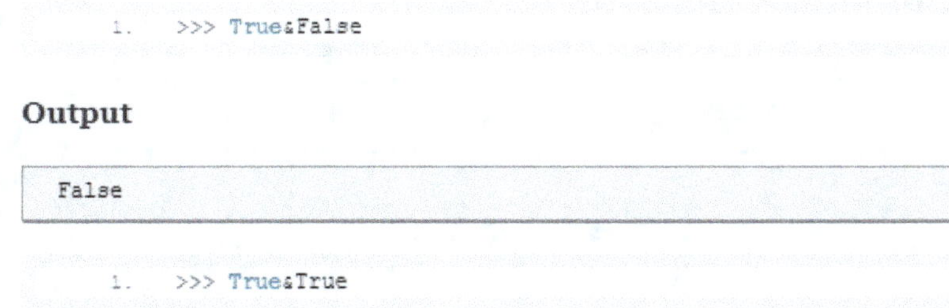

True

Because Booleans are single-bit, these operations are identical to applying them to 0 and/or Bitwise |

If both variables are False, it returns False.

>>> False|True

Output

True

Bitwise XOR (^)

This will only return True if one of the values is True and the other is False.

>>> **False^True**

Output

True

>>> **False^False**

Output

```
False
```

```
1.    >>> True^True
```

Output

```
False
```

Binary 1's Complement

This calculates 1's complement for True(1) and False(0).

>>> ~True

OUTPUT

```
-2
```

```
1.    >>> ~False
```

Output

```
-1
```

Left-shift(<<) and Right-shift(>>) Operators

As discussed earlier, these operators shift the value by specified number of bits left and right, respectively.

```
1.    >>> False>>2
2.    >>> True<<2
```

Output

4

One is true. When two places to the left are shifted, the result is 100, binary for four. As a result, it yields 4.

d. Identity

For Booleans, the identity operators 'is' and 'is not
applicable.

```
    1.    >>> False is False
```

Output

```
    True
```

```
    1.    >>> False is 0
```

Output

```
    False
```

e. Logical

Finally, logical operators work with Booleans.

>>> **False** and True

Output

False

This was all about the chapter on Python set and booleans.

Sets and Booleans are discussed in Python interview questions.

1. What is a Boolean expression in Python?
2. How do you check if a value is a Boolean, In Python?
3. In Python, how can you set a Boolean value?
4. Can you give an example of a Python set and a Boolean expression?
5. What is the best way to use Boolean in Python?

Chapter 5. FROZENSET

Python frozenset()

The frozenset() function creates an immutable frozenset object from the specified iterable's elements.

A frozen set is a Python set object that is immutable. While parts of a set can be changed at any moment, elements of a frozen set don't change after they've been created.

As a result, frozen sets can be used as Dictionary keys or as elements of other sets. However, it is not organized in the same way that sets are (the elements can be set at any index).

The frozenset() function has the following syntax:

```
frozenset([iterable])
```

frozenset() Parameters

There is only one parameter to the frozenset() function:

- iterable (Optional) - the iterable holds the elements that should be used to initialize the frozenset.

Set, dictionary, tuple, and other types of iterables exist.

Return value from frozenset()

The frozenset() function creates an immutable frozenset from the specified iterable's items.

It returns an empty frozenset if no arguments are supplied.

Example 1: Working of Python frozenset()

```python
# tuple of vowels
vowels = ('a', 'e', 'i', 'o', 'u')


fSet = frozenset(vowels)
print('The frozen set is:', fSet)
print('The empty frozen set is:', frozenset())


# frozensets are immutable
fSet.add('v')
```

Output

```
The frozen set is: frozenset({'a', 'o', 'u', 'i', 'e'})
The empty frozen set is: frozenset()
Traceback (most recent call last):
  File "<string>, line 8, in <module>
    fSet.add('v')
AttributeError: 'frozenset' object has no attribute 'add'
```

Example 2: Dictionary frozenset()

When you're using a dictionary as just an iterable for a frozen set, just the dictionary's keys are used to generate the set.

```python
# random dictionary
person = {"name": "John", "age": 23, "sex": "male"}

fSet = frozenset(person)
print('The frozen set is:', fSet)
```

Output

```
The frozen set is: frozenset({'name', 'sex', 'age'})
```

Frozenset operations

Like normal sets, frozenset can perform several operations
like copy, difference, symmetric_difference, intersection, and union.

```python
# Frozensets
# initialize A and B
A = frozenset([1, 2, 3, 4])
B = frozenset([3, 4, 5, 6])

# copying a frozenset
C = A.copy()  # Output: frozenset({1, 2, 3, 4})
print(C)

# union
print(A.union(B))  # Output: frozenset({1, 2, 3, 4, 5, 6})

# intersection
print(A.intersection(B))  # Output: frozenset({3, 4})

# difference
print(A.difference(B))  # Output: frozenset({1, 2})

# symmetric_difference
print(A.symmetric_difference(B))  # Output: frozenset({1, 2, 5, 6})
```

Output

```
frozenset({1, 2, 3, 4})
frozenset({1, 2, 3, 4, 5, 6})
frozenset({3, 4})
frozenset({1, 2})
frozenset({1, 2, 5, 6})
```

Similarly, other set techniques like issubset, isdisjoint, and issuperset are also available.

```python
# Frozensets
# initialize A, B and C
A = frozenset([1, 2, 3, 4])
B = frozenset([3, 4, 5, 6])
C = frozenset([5, 6])

# isdisjoint() method
print(A.isdisjoint(C))  # Output: True

# issubset() method
print(C.issubset(B))  # Output: True

# issuperset() method
print(B.issuperset(C))  # Output: True
```

Output

```
True
True
True
```

Chapter 6.
DICTIONARIES AND TUPLES

Tuples and Dictionaries

Python provides two more data structures that may store numerous objects in addition to lists. Dictionaries and tuples are the data structures in question. First, we'll talk about tuples.

Tuples

Tuples are lists that can't be changed. A list's elements can be changed, but a tuple's elements can only be accessed, not changed. The term tuple does not imply that this data structure may only hold two values.

In Python, tuples are created by enclosing components in parenthesis ( ) and separating them with commas. The following statement creates a tuple using the integers 3, 4, and 5.

```
>>> t_var = (3,4,5)
>>> t_var
(3, 4, 5)
```

Take note of how a list's elements can be changed:

```
>>> l_var = [3,4,5]  # a list
>>> l_var[0]= 8
>>> l_var
[8, 4, 5]
```

A tuple's elements cannot be updated. An error is returned if you try to assign a new value to one of the elements in a tuple.

```
>>> t_var = (3,4,5)  # a tuple

>>> t_var[0]= 8

>>> t_var
```

The 'tuple' object does not permit item assignment, which is a TypeError.
To create a tuple with only one numerical value, the number must be followed by a comma. If there is no comma, the variable is defined as a number.

```
>>> num = (5)

>>> type(num)

Int
```

The variable is classified as a tuple when a comma is added after the number.

```
>>> t_var = (5,)

>>> type(t_var)

tuple
```

Dictionaries

Key: value pairs are the building blocks of dictionaries. Lists and tuples are arranged and retrieved in Python based on their position. Keys and values are used to structure and retrieve dictionaries in Python. It doesn't matter where a pair of keys and values in a Python dictionary is kept.

Curly brackets are used to define dictionaries in Python. Commas separate the key-value pairs that make up the dictionary. A colon: connects each key-value pair.

Let's put two people's ages in a dictionary. Gabby and Maelle are the two individuals. Gabby is eight years old, and Maelle is five. It's worth noting that Gabby's name is a string and her age is an integer.

```
>>> age_dict = {"Gabby": 8 , "Maelle": 5}
>>> type(age_dict)
dict
```

The values stored in a dictionary are called and assigned using the following syntax:

```
dict_name[key] = value
>>> age_dict = {"Gabby": 8 , "Maelle": 5}
>>> age_dict["Gabby"]
```

We can add a new person to our age_dict with the following command:

```
>>> age_dict = {"Gabby": 8 , "Maelle": 5}
>>> age_dict["Peter"]= 40
>>> age_dict
{'Gabby': 8, 'Maelle': 5, 'Peter': 40}
```

Dictionaries can be converted to lists by calling the .items(), .keys(), and .values() techniques.

```
>>> age_dict = {"Gabby": 8 , "Maelle": 5}
>>> whole_list = list(age_dict.items())
>>> whole_list
[('Gabby', 8), ('Maelle', 5)]
>>> name_list = list(age_dict.keys())
>>> name_list
['Gabby', 'Maelle']
>>> age_list = list(age_dict.values())
>>> age_list
[8, 5]
```

The. pop() technique can be used to remove items from dictionaries. The dictionary key supplied to the. pop() technique (together with its associated value) is removed from the dictionary.

```
>>> age_dict = {"Gabby": 8 , "Maelle": 5}
>>> age_dict.pop("Gabby")
>>> age_dict
{'Maelle': 5}
```

CONCLUSION

Now that you have learned the main commands of Python, I recommend that you practice a lot and practice as much as possible so that you can make all the concepts explained in this guide your own.

Once you feel you are well versed and ready, you can start exploring more complex Python commands. At that point, nothing is off-limits because the great thing about Python is that it lets you do just about anything!

If you'd like to check out the other books in the series, you'll find more guides to help you along the way:

- **GET STARTED PROGRAMMING WITH PYTHON**
- **ADVANCED PYTHON COMMANDS**
- **PYTHON PRACTICAL APPLICATIONS and**
- **PYTHON TUTORIALS.**